50 Lemon and Lime Cooking Dishes

By: Kelly Johnson

Table of Contents

- Lemon Chicken
- Key Lime Pie
- Lemon Meringue Pie
- Lemon Risotto
- Lime Cilantro Rice
- Lemon Sorbet
- Lemon Garlic Shrimp
- Lemon Bars
- Lime Coconut Cake
- Lemon Vinaigrette
- Lemon Basil Pasta
- Lime Margarita
- Lemon-Glazed Salmon
- Lemon Pound Cake
- Lime Chicken Tacos
- Lemon Poppy Seed Muffins
- Lemonade
- Lime Curd
- Lemon Chicken Piccata

- Lime and Avocado Salad
- Lemon Drizzle Cake
- Lemon Ice Cream
- Lemon Ginger Chicken
- Lime Cheesecake
- Lemon-Infused Olive Oil
- Lime and Cilantro Grilled Fish
- Lemon and Garlic Roasted Potatoes
- Lime Jello Shots
- Lemon Curd Tart
- Lime Popsicles
- Lemon Pudding
- Lemonade Scones
- Lime and Ginger Chicken Wings
- Lemon-Glazed Carrots
- Key Lime Cheesecake
- Lime and Coconut Shrimp
- Lemon-Honey Chicken
- Lime and Mint Mojito
- Lemon Cucumber Salad
- Lemon and Garlic Butter Pasta

- Lime-Chili Chicken Skewers
- Lemon-Infused Water
- Lime and Coconut Rice Pudding
- Lemon-Butter Scallops
- Lime and Basil Sorbet
- Lemon-Spinach Quinoa
- Lime Cilantro Grilled Chicken
- Lemon Raspberry Tart
- Lime Marinated Pork
- Lemon Tofu Stir-Fry

Lemon Chicken

Ingredients:

- 4 boneless, skinless chicken breasts
- 2 tbsp olive oil
- Juice and zest of 2 lemons
- 3 garlic cloves, minced
- 1 tsp dried oregano
- 1 tsp thyme
- Salt and pepper to taste
- Fresh parsley, chopped (for garnish)

Instructions:

1. In a bowl, combine the lemon juice, zest, garlic, oregano, thyme, salt, and pepper.
2. Marinate the chicken breasts in the lemon mixture for at least 30 minutes.
3. Heat olive oil in a large skillet over medium heat.
4. Cook the chicken breasts for 6-7 minutes per side, until golden brown and cooked through.
5. Garnish with fresh parsley and serve.

Key Lime Pie

Ingredients:

- 1 1/2 cups graham cracker crumbs
- 1/4 cup sugar
- 1/2 cup melted butter
- 3 large egg yolks
- 1 can (14 oz) sweetened condensed milk
- 1/2 cup fresh key lime juice
- 1 tsp lime zest
- Whipped cream for topping

Instructions:

1. Preheat the oven to 350°F (175°C).
2. Mix the graham cracker crumbs, sugar, and melted butter. Press the mixture into the bottom of a pie dish to form the crust.
3. Bake the crust for 10 minutes, then let it cool.
4. In a bowl, whisk together the egg yolks, sweetened condensed milk, lime juice, and zest.
5. Pour the lime mixture into the cooled crust and bake for 15 minutes.
6. Let the pie cool, then refrigerate for at least 4 hours.
7. Top with whipped cream before serving.

Lemon Meringue Pie

Ingredients:

- 1 pre-baked pie crust
- 1 1/2 cups sugar
- 1/4 cup cornstarch
- 1/4 tsp salt
- 1 1/2 cups water
- 3 large egg yolks
- 2 tbsp butter
- 1/2 cup fresh lemon juice
- 1 tbsp lemon zest
- 3 large egg whites
- 1/4 tsp cream of tartar
- 6 tbsp sugar

Instructions:

1. Preheat the oven to 350°F (175°C).
2. In a saucepan, whisk together sugar, cornstarch, salt, and water. Cook over medium heat, stirring constantly, until the mixture thickens.
3. Whisk in egg yolks, butter, lemon juice, and lemon zest.
4. Pour the mixture into the pre-baked pie crust.
5. Beat the egg whites and cream of tartar until soft peaks form. Gradually add sugar and continue beating until stiff peaks form.
6. Spread the meringue over the lemon filling, ensuring it touches the crust.

7. Bake for 10-12 minutes, or until the meringue is golden.

8. Let the pie cool before serving.

Lemon Risotto

Ingredients:

- 1 tbsp olive oil
- 1 small onion, diced
- 1 1/2 cups Arborio rice
- 1/2 cup white wine
- 4 cups chicken or vegetable broth, kept warm
- Juice and zest of 1 lemon
- 1/2 cup grated Parmesan cheese
- Salt and pepper to taste

Instructions:

1. Heat the olive oil in a large pan over medium heat. Add the onion and cook until soft.
2. Stir in the rice and cook for 2 minutes.
3. Add the white wine and cook until absorbed.
4. Gradually add the warm broth, 1/2 cup at a time, stirring constantly until the liquid is absorbed before adding more.
5. Continue until the rice is tender and creamy (about 18 minutes).
6. Stir in the lemon juice, zest, and Parmesan. Season with salt and pepper, then serve.

Lime Cilantro Rice

Ingredients:

- 1 cup basmati rice
- 2 cups water
- 1 tbsp olive oil
- Juice and zest of 1 lime
- 1/4 cup fresh cilantro, chopped
- Salt to taste

Instructions:

1. Cook the rice according to package instructions.
2. In a large bowl, combine the cooked rice with olive oil, lime juice, zest, cilantro, and salt.
3. Stir well and serve.

Lemon Sorbet

Ingredients:

- 1 1/2 cups fresh lemon juice (about 6-8 lemons)
- 1 cup sugar
- 2 cups water

Instructions:

1. In a saucepan, combine the sugar and water over medium heat, stirring until the sugar dissolves.
2. Remove from heat and let cool to room temperature.
3. Stir in the lemon juice.
4. Pour the mixture into an ice cream maker and churn according to the manufacturer's instructions.
5. Transfer to a container and freeze until firm.

Lemon Garlic Shrimp

Ingredients:

- 1 lb large shrimp, peeled and deveined
- 2 tbsp olive oil
- 3 garlic cloves, minced
- Juice of 1 lemon
- 1/4 tsp red pepper flakes
- Salt and pepper to taste
- Fresh parsley, chopped (for garnish)

Instructions:

1. Heat olive oil in a large skillet over medium heat.
2. Add the garlic and cook for 1 minute, until fragrant.
3. Add the shrimp and cook for 2-3 minutes per side until pink and cooked through.
4. Stir in the lemon juice, red pepper flakes, salt, and pepper.
5. Garnish with parsley and serve.

Lemon Bars

Ingredients:

- **Crust:**
    - 1 cup all-purpose flour
    - 1/4 cup powdered sugar
    - 1/2 cup unsalted butter, softened
- **Filling:**
    - 1 cup granulated sugar
    - 2 tbsp all-purpose flour
    - 1/4 tsp baking powder
    - 2 large eggs
    - Juice of 2 lemons
    - 1/4 cup powdered sugar (for dusting)

Instructions:

1. Preheat the oven to 350°F (175°C).
2. For the crust, mix the flour, powdered sugar, and butter until crumbly. Press into the bottom of a greased 9x9-inch baking dish.
3. Bake for 15 minutes, then remove from the oven.
4. For the filling, whisk together the granulated sugar, flour, baking powder, eggs, and lemon juice.
5. Pour the filling over the baked crust and bake for an additional 20-25 minutes, until set.
6. Let cool completely, then dust with powdered sugar and cut into bars.

Lime Coconut Cake

Ingredients:

- 1 1/2 cups all-purpose flour
- 1 tsp baking powder
- 1/2 tsp salt
- 1/2 cup unsalted butter, softened
- 1 cup granulated sugar
- 3 large eggs
- 1/2 cup coconut milk
- Juice and zest of 2 limes
- 1/2 cup shredded coconut

Instructions:

1. Preheat the oven to 350°F (175°C). Grease and flour a 9-inch round cake pan.
2. In a bowl, whisk together flour, baking powder, and salt.
3. In another bowl, cream together butter and sugar until light and fluffy.
4. Beat in the eggs, one at a time, followed by the coconut milk, lime juice, and zest.
5. Gradually add the dry ingredients and mix until smooth.
6. Stir in the shredded coconut.
7. Pour the batter into the prepared pan and bake for 30-35 minutes, or until a toothpick comes out clean.
8. Let cool before serving.

Lemon Vinaigrette

Ingredients:

- 1/4 cup fresh lemon juice
- 1/2 cup olive oil
- 1 tsp Dijon mustard
- 1 tsp honey
- Salt and pepper to taste

Instructions:

1. Whisk together the lemon juice, olive oil, mustard, honey, salt, and pepper.
2. Drizzle over salads or roasted vegetables and serve.

Lemon Basil Pasta

Ingredients:

- 8 oz pasta (spaghetti or your choice)
- 2 tbsp olive oil
- 2 garlic cloves, minced
- Zest and juice of 2 lemons
- 1/2 cup fresh basil, chopped
- 1/4 cup grated Parmesan cheese
- Salt and pepper to taste

Instructions:

1. Cook the pasta according to package directions, then drain and set aside.
2. In a large skillet, heat the olive oil over medium heat and sauté the garlic until fragrant.
3. Add the lemon zest and juice to the skillet and stir to combine.
4. Toss the cooked pasta in the lemon mixture, then stir in the chopped basil and Parmesan.
5. Season with salt and pepper to taste, and serve immediately.

Lime Margarita

Ingredients:

- 2 oz lime juice (freshly squeezed)
- 2 oz tequila
- 1 oz orange liqueur (like Cointreau or triple sec)
- 1/2 oz simple syrup (or to taste)
- Salt (for rimming the glass)
- Lime wedge (for garnish)

Instructions:

1. Rim your glass with lime juice and dip it in salt.
2. In a cocktail shaker, combine lime juice, tequila, orange liqueur, and simple syrup.
3. Fill the shaker with ice and shake until well-chilled.
4. Strain the mixture into the prepared glass and garnish with a lime wedge.

Lemon-Glazed Salmon

Ingredients:

- 4 salmon fillets
- 1/4 cup fresh lemon juice
- 1 tbsp olive oil
- 2 tbsp honey
- 2 garlic cloves, minced
- Salt and pepper to taste
- Fresh parsley (for garnish)

Instructions:

1. Preheat the oven to 400°F (200°C).
2. In a small bowl, whisk together lemon juice, olive oil, honey, garlic, salt, and pepper.
3. Place the salmon fillets on a baking sheet and brush with the lemon glaze.
4. Bake for 12-15 minutes, until the salmon is cooked through.
5. Garnish with fresh parsley before serving.

Lemon Pound Cake

Ingredients:

- 1 1/2 cups all-purpose flour
- 1 tsp baking powder
- 1/4 tsp salt
- 1/2 cup unsalted butter, softened
- 1 cup granulated sugar
- 3 large eggs
- 1/2 cup sour cream
- Zest and juice of 2 lemons
- 1 tsp vanilla extract

Instructions:

1. Preheat the oven to 350°F (175°C). Grease and flour a loaf pan.
2. In a bowl, whisk together flour, baking powder, and salt.
3. In another bowl, cream the butter and sugar until light and fluffy.
4. Add the eggs one at a time, then mix in the sour cream, lemon zest, lemon juice, and vanilla.
5. Gradually add the dry ingredients and mix until smooth.
6. Pour the batter into the prepared pan and bake for 50-60 minutes, until a toothpick comes out clean.
7. Let cool in the pan before transferring to a wire rack.

Lime Chicken Tacos

Ingredients:

- 2 chicken breasts, cooked and shredded
- 1 tbsp olive oil
- 1 lime, juiced
- 1/2 tsp cumin
- 1/2 tsp chili powder
- Salt and pepper to taste
- Tortillas
- Toppings: diced avocado, cilantro, shredded cheese, sour cream, salsa

Instructions:

1. In a skillet, heat olive oil over medium heat.
2. Add the shredded chicken, lime juice, cumin, chili powder, salt, and pepper.
3. Cook for 5-7 minutes until the chicken is heated through and coated in the spices.
4. Serve the chicken in tortillas and top with your choice of toppings.

Lemon Poppy Seed Muffins

Ingredients:

- 1 3/4 cups all-purpose flour
- 1 tbsp poppy seeds
- 1 tsp baking powder
- 1/2 tsp baking soda
- 1/4 tsp salt
- 1/2 cup unsalted butter, softened
- 1 cup granulated sugar
- 2 large eggs
- 1/2 cup milk
- Zest of 2 lemons
- Juice of 1 lemon
- 1 tsp vanilla extract

Instructions:

1. Preheat the oven to 350°F (175°C) and line a muffin tin with paper liners.
2. In a bowl, whisk together flour, poppy seeds, baking powder, baking soda, and salt.
3. In another bowl, cream together butter and sugar until fluffy.
4. Beat in the eggs one at a time, then add the milk, lemon zest, lemon juice, and vanilla.
5. Gradually add the dry ingredients and mix until just combined.
6. Divide the batter evenly into the muffin cups and bake for 18-20 minutes, until a toothpick comes out clean.

Lemonade

Ingredients:

- 1 cup fresh lemon juice (about 4-6 lemons)
- 1 cup granulated sugar
- 5 cups water
- Ice cubes
- Lemon slices (for garnish)

Instructions:

1. In a small saucepan, combine 1 cup of water and the sugar. Heat until the sugar is dissolved to make a simple syrup.
2. In a pitcher, combine the lemon juice, simple syrup, and remaining 4 cups of water.
3. Stir well, then taste and adjust sweetness if needed.
4. Serve over ice with lemon slices for garnish.

Lime Curd

Ingredients:

- 1/2 cup fresh lime juice
- Zest of 2 limes
- 1/2 cup unsalted butter, cubed
- 3/4 cup granulated sugar
- 3 large eggs, beaten

Instructions:

1. In a medium saucepan, combine lime juice, lime zest, and sugar over medium heat. Stir to dissolve sugar.
2. Slowly whisk in the beaten eggs. Continue to cook, stirring constantly, until the mixture thickens (about 8-10 minutes).
3. Remove from heat and stir in the cubed butter until smooth.
4. Pour into a jar and refrigerate until cool. Serve with scones or toast.

Lemon Chicken Piccata

Ingredients:

- 4 boneless chicken breasts, flattened
- 1/2 cup all-purpose flour
- Salt and pepper to taste
- 2 tbsp olive oil
- 1/2 cup white wine
- 1/4 cup fresh lemon juice
- 2 tbsp capers, drained
- 1/4 cup fresh parsley, chopped

Instructions:

1. Season the chicken with salt and pepper, then dredge in flour.
2. In a skillet, heat olive oil over medium-high heat. Cook the chicken for 4-5 minutes per side, until golden brown and cooked through.
3. Remove the chicken and set aside.
4. In the same skillet, add wine, lemon juice, and capers. Simmer for 5 minutes.
5. Return the chicken to the skillet and coat in the sauce.
6. Garnish with parsley before serving.

Lime and Avocado Salad

Ingredients:

- 2 ripe avocados, diced
- 1 lime, juiced
- 1/4 cup red onion, finely chopped
- 1/2 cup cherry tomatoes, halved
- 1/4 cup cilantro, chopped
- Salt and pepper to taste

Instructions:

1. In a bowl, combine the avocado, lime juice, red onion, tomatoes, and cilantro.
2. Toss gently to combine, then season with salt and pepper.
3. Serve immediately as a fresh side salad or topping for tacos.

Lemon Drizzle Cake

Ingredients:

- 1 1/2 cups all-purpose flour
- 1 tsp baking powder
- 1/2 tsp baking soda
- 1/4 tsp salt
- 1/2 cup unsalted butter, softened
- 1 cup granulated sugar
- 2 large eggs
- 1/2 cup sour cream
- Zest and juice of 2 lemons
- 1 tsp vanilla extract
- 1/2 cup powdered sugar (for drizzle)

Instructions:

1. Preheat the oven to 350°F (175°C) and grease a loaf pan.
2. In a bowl, mix together the flour, baking powder, baking soda, and salt.
3. In another bowl, cream together the butter and sugar until light and fluffy.
4. Add the eggs one at a time, followed by the sour cream, lemon zest, lemon juice, and vanilla extract.
5. Gradually mix in the dry ingredients until smooth.
6. Pour the batter into the prepared pan and bake for 50-60 minutes, until a toothpick comes out clean.
7. In a small bowl, whisk together powdered sugar and lemon juice to make the drizzle.

8. Once the cake has cooled slightly, drizzle the glaze over the top. Let the cake cool completely before serving.

Lemon Ice Cream

Ingredients:

- 2 cups heavy cream
- 1 cup whole milk
- 3/4 cup granulated sugar
- Zest and juice of 2 lemons
- 1 tsp vanilla extract
- Pinch of salt

Instructions:

1. In a bowl, whisk together heavy cream, whole milk, sugar, lemon zest, lemon juice, vanilla extract, and a pinch of salt.

2. Pour the mixture into an ice cream maker and churn according to the manufacturer's instructions.

3. Once the ice cream has reached a soft-serve consistency, transfer it to a container and freeze for at least 4 hours.

4. Serve with extra lemon zest or a drizzle of lemon syrup, if desired.

Lemon Ginger Chicken

Ingredients:

- 4 boneless chicken breasts
- 2 tbsp olive oil
- 1 tbsp fresh ginger, grated
- 2 garlic cloves, minced
- Zest and juice of 1 lemon
- 2 tbsp soy sauce
- 1 tbsp honey
- Salt and pepper to taste

Instructions:

1. In a bowl, mix the olive oil, ginger, garlic, lemon zest, lemon juice, soy sauce, honey, salt, and pepper.
2. Marinate the chicken breasts in the mixture for at least 30 minutes (or overnight in the fridge for more flavor).
3. Preheat a skillet over medium heat and cook the chicken for 6-8 minutes per side, until fully cooked.
4. Serve the chicken with a side of vegetables or rice.

Lime Cheesecake

Ingredients:

- 1 1/2 cups graham cracker crumbs
- 1/4 cup sugar
- 1/3 cup unsalted butter, melted
- 3 packages (8 oz) cream cheese, softened
- 1 cup sour cream
- 1/2 cup granulated sugar
- 1/4 cup lime juice
- Zest of 2 limes
- 3 large eggs

Instructions:

1. Preheat the oven to 325°F (160°C).
2. Combine the graham cracker crumbs, sugar, and melted butter in a bowl. Press the mixture into the bottom of a greased 9-inch springform pan.
3. In a separate bowl, beat together cream cheese, sour cream, sugar, lime juice, and lime zest until smooth.
4. Add the eggs one at a time, mixing until just incorporated.
5. Pour the mixture over the crust and bake for 45-50 minutes, until the edges are set and the center is slightly jiggly.
6. Let the cheesecake cool, then refrigerate for at least 4 hours before serving.

Lemon-Infused Olive Oil

Ingredients:

- 1 cup extra virgin olive oil
- Zest of 2 lemons
- 1 sprig rosemary (optional)
- 1/2 tsp black peppercorns (optional)

Instructions:

1. In a small saucepan, combine the olive oil and lemon zest. Heat over low heat for 5-10 minutes, making sure it doesn't boil.
2. Remove from heat and let it cool to room temperature.
3. Add the rosemary and black peppercorns if using, then transfer to a clean bottle or jar.
4. Let the oil infuse for 3-5 days before using. It's great for drizzling over salads, vegetables, or grilled meats.

Lime and Cilantro Grilled Fish

Ingredients:

- 4 white fish fillets (such as cod or tilapia)
- Juice of 2 limes
- 1/4 cup fresh cilantro, chopped
- 2 garlic cloves, minced
- 2 tbsp olive oil
- Salt and pepper to taste

Instructions:

1. In a small bowl, whisk together lime juice, cilantro, garlic, olive oil, salt, and pepper.
2. Marinate the fish fillets in the mixture for at least 15 minutes.
3. Preheat the grill to medium heat and cook the fish for 4-5 minutes per side, until cooked through.
4. Serve with extra lime wedges and fresh cilantro.

Lemon and Garlic Roasted Potatoes

Ingredients:

- 1 1/2 lbs baby potatoes, halved
- 3 tbsp olive oil
- Zest and juice of 1 lemon
- 3 garlic cloves, minced
- Salt and pepper to taste
- Fresh parsley, chopped (for garnish)

Instructions:

1. Preheat the oven to 400°F (200°C).
2. In a bowl, toss the halved potatoes with olive oil, lemon zest, lemon juice, garlic, salt, and pepper.
3. Spread the potatoes in a single layer on a baking sheet.
4. Roast for 25-30 minutes, flipping halfway through, until golden and tender.
5. Garnish with fresh parsley before serving.

Lime Jello Shots

Ingredients:

- 1 box lime Jello (3 oz)
- 1 cup boiling water
- 1/2 cup cold water
- 1/2 cup tequila
- 1/4 cup lime juice
- 1/4 cup triple sec (optional)

Instructions:

1. Dissolve the lime Jello in boiling water, stirring until fully dissolved.
2. Add the cold water, tequila, lime juice, and triple sec (if using).
3. Pour the mixture into shot glasses and refrigerate for 2-3 hours, or until set.
4. Serve chilled with a salted rim if desired.

Lemon Curd Tart

Ingredients:

- 1 pre-baked tart shell (or homemade, if preferred)
- 1/2 cup lemon juice
- Zest of 2 lemons
- 1/2 cup granulated sugar
- 4 large eggs
- 1/2 cup unsalted butter, cubed

Instructions:

1. In a saucepan, whisk together lemon juice, lemon zest, sugar, and eggs.
2. Cook over medium heat, whisking constantly, until the mixture thickens (about 5 minutes).
3. Remove from heat and stir in the cubed butter until smooth.
4. Pour the lemon curd into the pre-baked tart shell and refrigerate for at least 2 hours before serving.

Lime Popsicles

Ingredients:

- 1 1/2 cups fresh lime juice (about 6 limes)
- 1 cup coconut milk
- 1/4 cup honey or agave syrup
- Zest of 2 limes

Instructions:

1. In a bowl, combine the lime juice, coconut milk, honey, and lime zest.
2. Pour the mixture into popsicle molds and insert sticks.
3. Freeze for 4-6 hours or until solid.
4. Run warm water over the outside of the molds to release the popsicles and serve.

Lemon Pudding

Ingredients:

- 1 cup whole milk
- 1/2 cup sugar
- 1/4 cup cornstarch
- 1/4 tsp salt
- 3 large egg yolks
- 2 tbsp unsalted butter
- Zest of 1 lemon
- 1/2 cup fresh lemon juice
- 1 tsp vanilla extract

Instructions:

1. In a saucepan, whisk together milk, sugar, cornstarch, and salt over medium heat.
2. Cook until the mixture thickens, stirring constantly.
3. In a separate bowl, whisk the egg yolks, then slowly add a bit of the hot milk mixture to temper the eggs.
4. Gradually add the egg mixture to the saucepan, stirring constantly.
5. Continue cooking for about 2-3 minutes, then remove from heat.
6. Stir in butter, lemon zest, lemon juice, and vanilla.
7. Pour into individual bowls or a large dish, and refrigerate for at least 2 hours before serving.

Lemonade Scones

Ingredients:

- 2 cups all-purpose flour
- 2 tbsp baking powder
- 1/2 cup sugar
- 1/2 tsp salt
- 1/2 cup cold unsalted butter, cubed
- 1/2 cup heavy cream
- 1/4 cup lemonade concentrate
- 1 egg (for egg wash)
- Powdered sugar for dusting

Instructions:

1. Preheat the oven to 400°F (200°C) and line a baking sheet with parchment paper.
2. In a large bowl, combine the flour, baking powder, sugar, and salt.
3. Cut in the cold butter until the mixture resembles coarse crumbs.
4. Stir in the cream and lemonade concentrate until just combined.
5. Turn the dough onto a floured surface and gently knead until smooth.
6. Roll out the dough to about 1-inch thickness and cut into triangles.
7. Place the scones on the prepared baking sheet, brush with a beaten egg, and bake for 15-18 minutes until golden brown.
8. Dust with powdered sugar and serve warm.

Lime and Ginger Chicken Wings

Ingredients:

- 12 chicken wings
- 2 tbsp fresh lime juice
- Zest of 1 lime
- 2 tbsp soy sauce
- 1 tbsp grated ginger
- 1 tbsp honey
- 2 garlic cloves, minced
- 1/2 tsp chili flakes (optional)
- Salt and pepper to taste

Instructions:

1. In a bowl, combine lime juice, lime zest, soy sauce, ginger, honey, garlic, chili flakes, salt, and pepper.
2. Marinate the chicken wings in the mixture for at least 1 hour.
3. Preheat the grill or oven to 400°F (200°C).
4. Grill or bake the wings for 25-30 minutes, flipping halfway through, until golden and cooked through.
5. Serve with extra lime wedges for squeezing.

Lemon-Glazed Carrots

Ingredients:

- 1 lb carrots, peeled and sliced
- 2 tbsp butter
- 2 tbsp honey
- Zest and juice of 1 lemon
- Salt and pepper to taste
- Fresh parsley, chopped (for garnish)

Instructions:

1. Cook the carrots in boiling salted water for 6-8 minutes, or until tender.
2. Drain and set aside.
3. In a skillet, melt the butter and honey over medium heat.
4. Add the lemon zest, juice, and salt and pepper, stirring to combine.
5. Toss the cooked carrots in the lemon glaze and cook for an additional 2-3 minutes.
6. Garnish with fresh parsley before serving.

Key Lime Cheesecake

Ingredients:

- 1 1/2 cups graham cracker crumbs
- 1/4 cup sugar
- 1/3 cup unsalted butter, melted
- 3 packages (8 oz) cream cheese, softened
- 1 cup sour cream
- 1/2 cup granulated sugar
- 3 large eggs
- 1/2 cup key lime juice
- Zest of 1 lime

Instructions:

1. Preheat the oven to 325°F (160°C).
2. Combine the graham cracker crumbs, sugar, and melted butter, then press into the bottom of a greased 9-inch springform pan.
3. In a separate bowl, beat together the cream cheese, sour cream, sugar, eggs, key lime juice, and lime zest until smooth.
4. Pour the mixture over the crust and bake for 45-50 minutes, or until set.
5. Let the cheesecake cool, then refrigerate for at least 4 hours.
6. Serve with extra lime zest or a lime garnish.

Lime and Coconut Shrimp

Ingredients:

- 1 lb large shrimp, peeled and deveined
- 1/2 cup coconut milk
- Zest and juice of 2 limes
- 2 tbsp honey
- 1 tbsp soy sauce
- 1/4 cup shredded coconut, toasted
- Salt and pepper to taste

Instructions:

1. In a bowl, combine coconut milk, lime zest, lime juice, honey, soy sauce, salt, and pepper.
2. Marinate the shrimp in the mixture for 20-30 minutes.
3. Heat a skillet over medium-high heat and cook the shrimp for 2-3 minutes per side, until pink and cooked through.
4. Sprinkle with toasted shredded coconut before serving.

Lemon-Honey Chicken

Ingredients:

- 4 boneless chicken breasts
- 2 tbsp olive oil
- Zest and juice of 1 lemon
- 2 tbsp honey
- 2 garlic cloves, minced
- 1 tsp dried thyme
- Salt and pepper to taste

Instructions:

1. In a bowl, whisk together lemon zest, lemon juice, honey, garlic, thyme, salt, and pepper.
2. Marinate the chicken breasts in the mixture for at least 30 minutes.
3. Heat olive oil in a skillet over medium heat and cook the chicken for 6-8 minutes per side, until fully cooked.
4. Serve the chicken with a drizzle of the leftover marinade.

Lime and Mint Mojito

Ingredients:

- 2 oz white rum
- 1 oz lime juice
- 1 tsp sugar (or simple syrup)
- 8-10 fresh mint leaves
- Club soda
- Ice
- Lime wedges for garnish

Instructions:

1. In a glass, muddle the mint leaves with sugar and lime juice.
2. Add the rum and fill the glass with ice.
3. Top with club soda and stir well.
4. Garnish with a lime wedge and extra mint leaves.

Lemon Cucumber Salad

Ingredients:

- 1 cucumber, thinly sliced
- 1/4 red onion, thinly sliced
- 1/2 cup crumbled feta cheese
- 1/4 cup fresh dill, chopped
- Zest and juice of 1 lemon
- 2 tbsp olive oil
- Salt and pepper to taste

Instructions:

1. In a bowl, combine cucumber, onion, feta, and dill.
2. In a separate small bowl, whisk together lemon zest, lemon juice, olive oil, salt, and pepper.
3. Pour the dressing over the salad and toss to combine.
4. Serve chilled.

Lemon and Garlic Butter Pasta

Ingredients:

- 8 oz pasta (spaghetti or fettuccine)
- 3 tbsp unsalted butter
- 4 garlic cloves, minced
- Zest and juice of 1 lemon
- 1/4 cup grated Parmesan cheese
- Salt and pepper to taste
- Fresh parsley, chopped (for garnish)

Instructions:

1. Cook pasta according to package instructions and drain, reserving 1/2 cup of pasta water.
2. In a large skillet, melt butter over medium heat and sauté garlic until fragrant.
3. Add lemon zest, lemon juice, and pasta water to the skillet. Stir to combine.
4. Toss the cooked pasta into the skillet and mix until well coated.
5. Stir in Parmesan cheese and season with salt and pepper.
6. Garnish with fresh parsley and serve.

Lime-Chili Chicken Skewers

Ingredients:

- 4 boneless chicken breasts, cut into chunks
- 2 tbsp lime juice
- Zest of 1 lime
- 1 tbsp chili powder
- 1 tsp cumin
- 1 tbsp olive oil
- 1 tsp garlic powder
- Salt and pepper to taste
- Wooden skewers (soaked in water for 30 minutes)

Instructions:

1. In a bowl, combine lime juice, lime zest, chili powder, cumin, olive oil, garlic powder, salt, and pepper.
2. Add the chicken chunks to the marinade and refrigerate for at least 1 hour.
3. Preheat the grill or grill pan to medium-high heat.
4. Thread the marinated chicken onto the skewers.
5. Grill the skewers for 6-8 minutes per side until the chicken is cooked through.
6. Serve with lime wedges for extra flavor.

Lemon-Infused Water

Ingredients:

- 1 lemon, sliced
- 4 cups cold water
- Ice cubes

Instructions:

1. In a pitcher, add lemon slices and cold water.
2. Stir gently and refrigerate for at least 1 hour to allow the lemon to infuse the water.
3. Serve over ice and enjoy as a refreshing, low-calorie drink.

Lime and Coconut Rice Pudding

Ingredients:

- 1 cup Arborio rice
- 4 cups coconut milk
- 1/2 cup sugar
- 1/2 tsp vanilla extract
- Zest of 1 lime
- 1/4 cup lime juice
- Pinch of salt

Instructions:

1. In a large saucepan, combine rice, coconut milk, sugar, and salt.
2. Bring to a simmer over medium heat, stirring occasionally.
3. Cook for 25-30 minutes, until the rice is tender and the mixture has thickened.
4. Remove from heat and stir in vanilla, lime zest, and lime juice.
5. Serve warm or chilled, topped with toasted coconut flakes or fresh fruit.

Lemon-Butter Scallops

Ingredients:

- 12 large sea scallops, patted dry
- 2 tbsp unsalted butter
- 2 garlic cloves, minced
- Zest and juice of 1 lemon
- 1 tbsp fresh parsley, chopped
- Salt and pepper to taste

Instructions:

1. Heat a large skillet over medium-high heat and melt butter.
2. Add the scallops to the skillet, cooking for 2-3 minutes per side until golden brown and cooked through.
3. Remove the scallops from the skillet and set aside.
4. Add garlic to the skillet and sauté for 1 minute until fragrant.
5. Add lemon juice, lemon zest, and parsley. Stir to combine.
6. Return the scallops to the skillet and toss to coat in the sauce.
7. Serve immediately, garnished with extra parsley.

Lime and Basil Sorbet

Ingredients:

- 1 cup fresh lime juice
- 1/2 cup sugar
- 1 cup water
- 1/4 cup fresh basil leaves, chopped

Instructions:

1. In a saucepan, combine water and sugar. Heat over medium heat, stirring until sugar dissolves.
2. Remove from heat and let cool.
3. Stir in lime juice and basil, then transfer the mixture to a blender and blend until smooth.
4. Pour the mixture into a shallow dish and freeze for 3-4 hours, stirring every 30 minutes to prevent ice crystals.
5. Once fully frozen, serve the sorbet in bowls or scoops.

Lemon-Spinach Quinoa

Ingredients:

- 1 cup quinoa, rinsed
- 2 cups vegetable broth or water
- 2 tbsp olive oil
- 1 garlic clove, minced
- 3 cups fresh spinach, chopped
- Zest and juice of 1 lemon
- Salt and pepper to taste

Instructions:

1. In a medium saucepan, bring vegetable broth or water to a boil.
2. Add quinoa, reduce heat to low, and cover. Cook for 15 minutes, until the quinoa is tender and the liquid is absorbed.
3. In a skillet, heat olive oil over medium heat and sauté garlic until fragrant.
4. Add spinach to the skillet and cook until wilted.
5. Stir in cooked quinoa, lemon zest, and lemon juice.
6. Season with salt and pepper and serve.

Lime Cilantro Grilled Chicken

Ingredients:

- 4 boneless chicken breasts
- 1/4 cup lime juice
- Zest of 1 lime
- 2 tbsp olive oil
- 2 garlic cloves, minced
- 1/4 cup fresh cilantro, chopped
- Salt and pepper to taste

Instructions:

1. In a bowl, whisk together lime juice, lime zest, olive oil, garlic, cilantro, salt, and pepper.
2. Marinate the chicken breasts in the mixture for at least 1 hour.
3. Preheat the grill to medium-high heat.
4. Grill the chicken for 6-8 minutes per side, or until fully cooked.
5. Serve with extra cilantro for garnish.

Lemon Raspberry Tart

Ingredients:

- 1 pre-baked tart shell (or homemade, if preferred)
- 1/2 cup fresh lemon juice
- Zest of 2 lemons
- 1/2 cup sugar
- 4 large eggs
- 1/2 cup fresh raspberries
- 1 tbsp cornstarch (optional, for thickening)

Instructions:

1. In a bowl, whisk together lemon juice, lemon zest, sugar, and eggs.
2. Pour the mixture into the tart shell and bake at 325°F (160°C) for 20-25 minutes, or until set.
3. Let cool completely.
4. In a small saucepan, combine raspberries and sugar. Cook over medium heat until the raspberries break down.
5. If using cornstarch, dissolve it in water and add to the raspberry mixture to thicken.
6. Once the tart is cool, top with raspberry sauce and serve.

Lime Marinated Pork

Ingredients:

- 4 pork chops
- 1/4 cup lime juice
- 2 tbsp olive oil
- 2 garlic cloves, minced
- 1 tsp ground cumin
- 1/4 cup fresh cilantro, chopped
- Salt and pepper to taste

Instructions:

1. In a bowl, whisk together lime juice, olive oil, garlic, cumin, cilantro, salt, and pepper.
2. Marinate the pork chops in the mixture for at least 30 minutes.
3. Preheat the grill or skillet to medium-high heat.
4. Grill the pork chops for 4-5 minutes per side, or until cooked through.
5. Serve with extra cilantro and lime wedges.

Lemon Tofu Stir-Fry

Ingredients:

- 1 block firm tofu, pressed and cubed
- 2 tbsp sesame oil
- 1 red bell pepper, sliced
- 1 carrot, julienned
- 1 zucchini, sliced
- 2 tbsp soy sauce
- 1 tbsp lemon juice
- 1 tsp grated ginger
- 1 tsp honey (optional)
- Fresh cilantro for garnish

Instructions:

1. In a skillet, heat sesame oil over medium heat.
2. Add tofu cubes and cook until golden brown, about 5-7 minutes.
3. Remove tofu and set aside.
4. In the same skillet, sauté bell pepper, carrot, and zucchini until tender, about 5 minutes.
5. In a small bowl, whisk together soy sauce, lemon juice, ginger, and honey.
6. Return tofu to the skillet and pour the sauce over it. Toss to coat and cook for 2 more minutes.
7. Garnish with fresh cilantro and serve.

www.ingramcontent.com/pod-product-compliance
Lightning Source LLC
LaVergne TN
LVHW081322060526
838201LV00055B/2408